# transport
## around the world

## Godfrey Hall

**Wayland**

## Titles in this series:
Clothes Around the World
Festivals Around the World
Food Around the World
Houses Around the World
Musical Instruments Around the World
Shops and Markets Around the World
Toys and Games Around the World
Transport Around the World

With thanks to Sue my wife, Hicham Ennami, Mike Theobald, Madeline Murphy, Joan and Harold Vidler.

Series editor: Deb Elliott
Book design: Malcolm Walker
Cover design: Simon Balley

First published in 1995 by
Wayland (Publishers) Limited
61 Western Road, Hove
East Sussex BN3 1JD

**British Library Cataloguing in Publication Data**
Hall, Godfrey
    Transport. – (Around the World Series)
    I. Title II. Series
    388
ISBN 0 7502 1245 4

Typeset by Kudos Design Services
Printed and bound by Rotolito Lombarda S.p.A.

**Acknowledgements**
The publishers would like to thank the following for allowing their pictures to be reproduced in this book: Eye Ubiquitous 13 (bottom, David Cumming), 17 (Tim Hawkins), 18 (top, Frank Leather), 20 (A. Carroll); Robert Harding Picture Library 14, 15, 19 (top); Impact contents page (Jorn Stjerneklar), 5 (Alan Keohane), 6 (Piers Cavendish), 13 (top, Mark Henley), 28 (Dingo/Erinhoult Features); Rex Features 12 (Patsy Fagan), 16, 22 (top, Chamussy) (bottom, Fotex/Drewa), 25 (Jeff Werner), 29 (Nigel Snowdon); Tony Stone Worldwide 5 (top, Sean Arbabi), 7 (bottom and cover, Chris Kapolka), 8 (bottom, Gene Lincoln), 9 and cover (Richard Brown), 10 (top and cover, Laurence Monneret), bottom (Paul Chesley), 11 (bottom and cover, David Hanson), 18 (bottom, Ed Pritchard), 19 (bottom, Don Spiro), 21 (Robert Cockburn), 23 (Matthew McVay), 24 (Chris Noble), 26 (Mark Snyder), 27 (Rex A. Butcher); Zul/Chapel Studios 5 (bottom, Graham Horner), 8 (top, Adam Good).

# Contents

# Our transport

All over the world people and goods are moving from place to place. Sometimes this is done by foot, but most of the time people use some form of transport.

In rough, mountain areas of Morocco, donkeys carry people along tracks which cars or trains cannot pass through.

Hot-air balloons can carry people across the sky.
It is a slow and expensive form of transport, but
it is great fun.

This vehicle has
enough power to
pull a boat out of
a lake.

# High-speed trains

The Eurostar is designed to travel through the Channel Tunnel from London to Paris, and from London to Brussels in Belgium. The train can travel at speeds of over 250 kilometres an hour.

The high speed trains in Japan are called Bullet trains. They are hardly ever late and travel at 200 kilometres an hour.

The TGV railway system links all the cities in France.

# Cold weather travel

In cold countries it is often not possible to use cars or trucks because of the snow and ice.

Snowmobiles travel across the snow on skis. These vehicles are powered by engines.

Snowploughs are used to clear roads and motorways after a heavy snowfall.

In America, children do not get a day off after a snowstorm. School buses are built to carry passengers in all weathers.

# Hot weather travel

In China and Singapore people sometimes travel in rickshaws. These are small, two-wheeled vehicles pulled by one or two people on foot, or someone on a bicycle.

People in the Philippines can travel around in colourful trucks called jeepnies.

Camels are used as
transport in very hot
desert areas, because
they can travel for a
long time without
water.

# Bicycles

Bicycles are cheap and easy to look after. In many countries, children travel to school on bicycles.

This three-wheeled cyclo is used to carry passengers in Phnom Penh in Kampuchea.

Holland is a flat country, so many people travel around on bicycle.

# Sailing boats

Sailing boats have been a means of transport for a long time.

Feluccas are used on the River Nile in Egypt.

In Hong Kong and China there are boats called
junks. These sailing boats have flat bottoms and
square sails.

# Seacraft

One of the most spectacular forms of sea transport is the catamaran. It zooms across the sea at great speed.

The hovercraft floats on a cushion of air and can travel on land or water. This hovercraft carries passengers across the Channel between England and France.

# Ferries

Ferries take goods,
cars and people across
water. This ferry is
crossing a lake in
Switzerland.

The Star Ferry travels
across Hong Kong
harbour.

Some villages in Mali, West Africa, are impossible to reach by road. Villagers use small ferry boats to cross rivers to other villages.

In New York, many people travel to work on the Staten Island ferry.

# Passenger planes

Large jet planes can take hundreds of people long distances. The pilots are very highly trained.

In parts of the world where there are no airports and there is a lot of water, people use seaplanes. These have special floats instead of wheels.

# Flying doctor

If you become sick and live a long way from a doctor then help may come to you by air.

In the Australian outback the Flying Doctor Service brings medical help to the sick.

Helicopter ambulances are used to help people on oil rigs and on boats.

An emergency helicopter searches for people lost in a forest.

# Private planes

Some people have their own private planes.

Here, in California in America, people with private planes are landing at an airpark alongside cars.

# Trams

A cable car carries passengers along Montgomery Street in San Francisco in California, America.

People travel around the city of Hong Kong in decorated trams. Trams are powered by electricity and run along rails in the road.

# Transport of the future

Car makers are always coming up with new, more modern and exciting types of car. This is one of the latest models.

This vehicle has special solar panels attached to it which use the sun's energy as power. Perhaps one day transport will use natural power, from the sun or plants, for example, rather than oil which pollutes the environment.

# Glossary

**cable car**   A car which is pulled by a large cable, usually up steep hills.

**camel**   An animal that can last a long time in the desert without food or water.

**environment**   Our surroundings.

**Eurostar**   A special train that is designed to travel at high speeds through the Channel Tunnel, linking cities in Europe.

**felucca**   A narrow ship with oars or sails, used in Egypt.

**outback**   The remote parts of Australia.

**pollutes**   Makes dirty or poisons.

**seaplane**   An aircraft that is able to land and take off on water. It does this using special floats.

**snowplough**   This is fitted to the front of vehicles to help move snow.

**solar panel**   A panel which turns the energy of the sun into electricity.

# Books to read

*Looking Back - Transport* Flynn (Wayland, 1991)

*A-Z Transport* Mathias and Thompson (Franklin Watts, 1988)

*Transport* Elliott (Wayland, 1993)

*Land and Sea Transport* Johnstone (Gloucester Press, 1989)

*World Transport, Travel and Communication* Knapp (Atlantic, 1994)

# More information

Would you like to know more about the people and places you have seen in the photographs in this book? If so, read on.

**contents page**
Zanzibar is an island off the east coast of Africa. The weather is warm all year round. Buses do not have windows, so passengers can have lots of fresh air to keep cool.

**Our transport**
Morocco is a kingdom in north-west Africa. It is mostly mountainous, with the Atlas Mountains in the centre and the Rif Mountains along the Mediterranean coast. The Sahara desert crosses the south and south-east of the country.
The air inside a hot-air balloon is heated by a flame which is in a large fabric bag. The warm air inside the balloon is lighter than the air outside which makes the balloon move.
This four-wheel drive vehicle gives the driver control of all four wheels at once. The photograph was taken at a loch in Scotland.

**High-speed trains**
The Eurostar trains carry passengers through the Channel Tunnel from London to Paris in three hours, and from London to Brussels in three hours and ten minutes.
A Japanese Bullet train with the snow-capped Mount Fuji in the background.
TGV stands for 'Train à Grande Vitesse', which literally means very fast train.

**Cold weather travel**
A man riding a snowmobile in Meribel, a popular ski resort in the French Alps.
Snowploughs scoop up snow and pack it out of the way at the side of the road or mountain path. Snowploughs are also used to clear ski slopes after a heavy snowfall.
A traditional yellow school bus taking children to school in Vermont, America.

**Hot weather travel**
A rickshaw driver reads his morning paper in Chinatown, Singapore.
A richly decorated jeepney used as passenger transport in Baguio, Philippines.
This police motorcycle has a sidecar for carrying passengers.
A Bedouin on a camel in Petra, Jordan.

**Bicycles**
Japanese children travelling to school on bicycles.
Buddhist monks being transported by cyclo in Phnom Penh, Kampuchea - the country known as Cambodia before 1976.
A mother carries her child on the front of a bicycle in Delft, Holland.

**Sailing boats**
Feluccas are narrow boats with tall sails. This felucca is on the River Nile at Aswan in Egypt.
A Chinese junk in full sail with Hong Kong island in the background.

**Seacraft**
Catamarans are sailing vessels with twin hulls held in place by a rigid framework.
Hovercraft travel on a cushion of air produced by fans.

**Ferries**
This ferry is carrying passengers across Lake Laman in Switzerland.
The famous Star Ferry is photographed here against the financial district of Hong Kong.
Mali is a republic in West Africa and is completely landlocked. The villagers in the photograph are crossing the River Niger at Segou.
Staten Island lies in New York Harbour. It is part of New York city.

**Passenger planes**
This jumbo jet belongs to TWA. It is coming in to land at Gatwick airport in England, bringing hundreds of passengers from America.
Seaplanes can take off and land on water.

**Flying doctor**
The Australian outback covers thousands of square kilometres of remote bush country. People living there need the flying doctor service to bring medical assistance, as it would take much too long to travel to hospital by car.
A helicopter bringing a medical team to help injured workers on an oil rig.
Emergency helicopters can look for people lost in mountains and forests much more quickly than people travelling by road.

**Private planes**
Two men struggle to move their small aircraft in Montreal, Canada. It is not unusual for rich Canadians and Americans to have their own private planes which they keep in garages.
Landing private planes at an airpark in Los Angeles. People can fly to work straight from home.

**Trams**
San Francisco is famous for its hilly streets and electronic cable cars which carry people around this northern Californian city.
The decorated trams in Hong Kong are a popular tourist attraction.

**Transport of the future**
The Renault Scenic, an innovative car designed to be ultra safe.
This solar-powered vehicle took part in the 1990 World Solar Challenge race.

# Index